SIDE BOOBS

DATING STORIES FROM A GENTLEMAN'S PERSPECTIVE

DU KIRPALANI

Cover design by www.wombonline.com
For updates please visit www.dukirpalani.com

ISBN-13: 978-0615957753
ISBN: 0615957757

SIDE BOOBS

DATING STORIES FROM A GENTLEMAN'S PERSPECTIVE

CONTENTS

ACKNOWLEDGMENTS

I have a few people to quickly thank; my mother for constantly telling me not to worry, despite raising me with constant panic in her voice. My grandfather for teaching me that the only thing that appreciates in value in this world is hard work. My sister for her words of encouragement when I need them. My second dysfunctional family or comedian friends for their supportive love and loyalty. A thank you to my friend Diane for being a friend and cheerleader to my writing. Insightful Olney, for her kindness and for helping me get this book to the next level. Each of you means the world to me and as a token of my gratitude, I must insist on a fifteen percent discount on any one of my books to you and your immediate family members.

TO THE READER

How does one find true love in a city that thrives on wearing masks? In Los Angeles, a city filled with people seeking fame or love from strangers, the world of dating can be confusing, crazy and even insulting at times. The book is 'Side Boobs', but there are many nights where I, the author, am the biggest boob in the room.

As a comedian and writer, I am very aware that I am far from perfect, flawed in many ways. There are days I just don't like anything about myself. There are days I feel unstoppable, polite and charming like George Clooney and strangely enough, those are the times I feel more like myself. I am by no means, 'a catch' in my opinion. I have great hair, kind eyes and that's about it.

What this book sets out to do is give you, the reader, an unfiltered view of the mind and heart of a young man on a date, in the hopes that you as a woman or a man, take it easier on yourself and who knows, maybe even your date.

I can only promise brutal honesty and a happy enough ending. This isn't a romantic comedy starring Anne Hathaway and Ryan Reynolds. It will, however, be true stories with real people who believe those certain stories and fairy tale endings can and will happen. As a hopeless romantic myself, I am one of them.

1 CASSIE

"I COULD LIKE TOTALLY quote you right now and come across intelligent," celebrated Cassie as she swatted my arm with jest. The awkward redheaded bombshell towered a full two inches over me and wore flat shoes like a boss. One could say the girl had the personality of a surprise birthday party. Cassie was an actress of course. Pre-type cast to be the awkward best friend and for what it's worth, I could see her on TV stealing the show in that type of role. There was a non-threatening big presence about Cassie.

As we flirted, I gave her enough room to feel confident and moments later Cassie inquired, "I know you probably don't care about the TV show 'Chuck', but I'm invited to a screening of this season's finale."

Before I could say anything, Cassie answered for me, "You probably don't watch Chuck, you're too smart for that show, it's cool, I just thought I'd ask, unless you want to go? Okay I'll stop talking. Do you want to go, like seriously, do you? It's like 'Chuck' so yeah, do you want to? Okay I'll stop talking for now. Okay, now. Your turn. Go."

I wouldn't take Cassie to an antique shop. I think her astonishment at the age of the artifacts would cause her to toss the objects up in the air. This was just a screening though. I really did need to get my mind of my ex-girlfriend and at this point in time, watching 'Chuck' at a sports bar with Hollywood schmoozers seemed like a good idea.

"Thanks for driving us, Du!" Cassie snickered as she buckled up her seat belt. I closed my car's passenger door on her gazing eyes and walked around to the driver's side. Half a moment later, I opened my door and the sounds of Cassie came flooding out, "Oh my god this is like a cassette stereo, in your car? Your car looks so new though! This is a Lexus right?" I didn't want to explain how a 1992 LS 400 was the closest to a reliable classic that I could afford now, so instead I just pushed in the cassette to entertain her mind. Sadly, it did. "No way, so that's like inside now and there are like things turning?" Cassie swooned. "Yeah, things turning," I added. I wanted to expand on analog technology, but her laughter cut me off. This was the precise time for me to pop the car into drive and hate myself from the inside.

Then again, who the hell was I to get in the way of this girl's lovely evening? How dare I judge her for being happy, excited and everything that I'm not? Cassie was nice enough to ask me out. She was nice enough to invite me to a private screening with free drinks. But seriously though, how old was this girl if a cassette tape amused her that much?

I sneakily checked her ID after we ordered drinks at the bar. Cassie was twenty four, or five years younger than me at the time. I began to think to myself; was I that much older than my own age? Why did twenty nine feel like bitterness toward anyone in their mid-twenties? Maybe I was just incredibly wise. And then I saw an angel. My mind started racing as I soaked in the sight of the gorgeous bartender. I did not, however, think about that bartender. My ex-girlfriend was a bartender. Way more beautiful and stunning than this bartender. I bet you this bartender never hides chocolate from herself in the kitchen. Really? Was I that much of a boob? I just wanted to move forward. Let it go man, let it go. Oh man, but this bartender just put ice cubes into a rocks glass in a very familiar manner. Perhaps, this meant that my ex-girlfriend was thinking of me as she tended bar elsewhere. "What are you thinking about?" interrupted Cassie. "Thinking? I was just admiring the giant screen behind the bartender," I replied like a sociopath, knowing that if I mentioned the hot bartender in the lie, I wouldn't be caught lying. I really had to stop comparing girls to my ex. It wasn't healthy and was wrong at all levels. "That is a nice screen behind the bar. You're so observant," Cassie calmly added. "I know right!" Why was I so good at being an asshole?

The sports bar on Melrose Avenue, unlike a college sports bar was designed simply and elegantly for a slightly older clientele. Tonight, the side room was comfortably packed for the screening. There were sixty people over-dressed in evening casuals and there wasn't one empty chair or barstool in sight. As the lights dimmed, patrons prepared themselves for the season finale of 'Chuck'.

The cold opening ambled along. There was a fake, heavy tension in the room as if we were all witnessing something monumental. It was 'Chuck.' This wasn't even the last episode of the series, just one of the later seasons. No one explained to me why this was a get-together and why everyone was dressed up. The cold opening ended with an over-sold cliff hanger moment. A massive applause broke out and a middle-aged man whistled to impress one of the pretty actresses in the room. She snickered, showed the man her naked shoulder and turned her gaze back toward the screen. The man nudged his friend and then took a swig of his vodka. This indicated that he was confident of hooking up at the end of the episode. If only life were that simple. "Did you like the opening?!" yelled Cassie as she grabbed my leg. "Yeah. I can't wait to see what happens after this Tide commercial." I replied.

The next hour was brutal. Mind you, I love television and can appreciate almost any show, but there's nothing worse than a bunch of phonies being phony together. I could sense call backs to jokes from earlier episodes getting only 5% of the room. To me this meant, the remaining 95% were pretending to be viewers of the show to either schmooze or lick boot with TV's elite. The episode ended on someone getting shot and the biggest plastic applause. The middle-aged man whistled loudly again, but this time, the young actress didn't turn around. Instead she yawned. This yawn was an opening for a younger gentleman wearing duck shoes who had just had his teeth cleaned. Duck shoes and the yawning actress began to flirt while the middle-aged man sadly glanced at the melted ice in his cocktail glass.

On our way out, Cassie introduced me to the director of the freshly viewed 'Chuck' episode. The man lit up when he saw Cassie in her sexy, emerald green dress. I was as sure that he had a crush on her, as he was old enough to be her dad. I could tell by his handshake with me that he didn't want me to exist. Part of me knew that Cassie partially invited me to let the director know that he didn't have a chance and she just wanted to be cast in some upcoming episode. I guess I was doing something nice for her on some level. I now wanted to do something nice for the director. I thought about introducing him to the other middle-aged man with melted ice. They both had so much in common.

They could smoke a cigar together and forget about their receding hairlines.

"Wasn't that awesome?" Cassie asked as we headed back to the car. "Yeah, I was surprised at how much fun I had," I answered, lying through my teeth. Cassie couldn't stop talking and I began to count steps to tune her out. "No. Stop being such an asshole." I thought to myself. "There were men in that bar, with power and money spanking it to the girl that asked *you* out on a date." By the time I opened the car door, I lost my step count. Cassie shyly smiled as I held my car's passenger door open for her. Then, like a lady from the nineteen fifties, she conservatively filled the seat and tucked her legs inside the car. It was in that moment where I realized, Cassie was a girl raised by a lady. I was nothing more than an asshole clinging on to bitterness.

Driving back I could only redeem myself by talking about whatever she wanted to. If there was anything I could give this girl, it would be a good conversation. "What do you think of Justin Bieber?" Cassie asked before I could pull the car out of its space. She then ironically turned down the volume of my 'Best of the Doors' playing on my cassette tape stereo as she now called it. "I've never met Justin Bieber so I really can't say anything," I replied. "No, of course you haven't met him, I mean, like, what do you think of his music?"

I didn't want to offend her, nor Bieber. "I think

we're all great at something and Justin Bieber found what he's great at." The silence was deafening. Was she going to flip out? Cassie held her hands in front of her face. This was the longest silence of the entire evening. She then closed the tips of her fingers like an Italian chef and kissed them. "Wow, just wow," she said aloud to herself. What just happened? I didn't feel shy to speak my mind so I asked her, "What just happened?"

I felt Cassie's gaze on the side of my face and she said, "You say these little gems and I just want to write them down as quotes." It was very nice of her to speak from her heart. Cassie's car was parked outside my apartment. I kissed her goodnight. I just didn't want to leave her hanging. It wouldn't be nice. Two days later, I had sex with Cassie. I just didn't want to leave her hanging. It wouldn't be nice.

As sexy as she was, and as adorable as she was as a person, I just couldn't connect with someone that was so much happier than me. I know I shouldn't have had sex with her, but I felt bad for all the middle-aged men who couldn't sleep with her and I felt bad that I didn't make as much money as their nannies did. Why was I turning into an asshole? I didn't know.

I apologized to Cassie three days later. She asked if I was still in love with my ex and I replied, "No I'm over her, I'm just trying to get over myself." I could hear Cassie thinking over the phone.

2 HAILEY

HAILEY CLIMAXED HARD ENOUGH, loud enough and enough times for the neighbors and their partially deaf dog, Zoey to hear. When I rolled off Hailey's sweaty body, the only audible sound in my bedroom was the slow burning crackle from my cigarette. The moment sex was over I wanted to be alone with my guilt. I just wanted her to leave and not ask any questions. "I hope I'm not just a rebound," stated Hailey as I choked on my second drag.

Hailey had perfect timing, but apparently no memory whatsoever. Her statement about being a rebound made absolutely no sense to me at all. In fact, our conversation on Facebook hours earlier was her asking me out for a drink, followed by my telling her, I didn't feel like going out because my girlfriend and I recently broke up, followed by *her* message saying, if I didn't feel like going out, that she could come over and cheer me up, followed by her final message which was a winky face emoticon. I'm no expert at linguistics, but to me this was a girl offering rebound sex.

I don't know why I said yes to such an offer, but at the time I was willing to do anything to move on so I could look for love again. Was I supposed to remind Hailey of her facebook messages? I couldn't. I'm not going to call someone out on their shit while they're naked in bed. I had to say something though. "Why bring this up now?" I responded. "You're right. Can we watch one of your Smallville DVDs?" Hailey gazed at me with her vampire-esque qualities. Her pupils were dark and large, her skin pale and her body, agile as fuck. If you asked me what I saw her in, I would take a long moment and then ask to be excused. Looking back today, I know I wasn't the one taking advantage of a girl that didn't know what she was doing. This was a girl who wanted to take advantage of a guy clearly in a vulnerable state. Hailey knew she would get incredible sex from someone who currently hated themselves.

I politely informed Hailey that I would have watched Smallville with her, but I wasn't in the mood for TV and shit. The truth was those Smallville DVDs, nine seasons of them were something my ex and I bought, watched and shared together as we cuddled on the couch sipping flower or fruit flavored teas. Tonight, Hailey had experienced my body, but she could never share my Smallville. This was the pathetic thought I had in my mind. Hailey resumed talking and the sound of her voice bothered me immensely. I usually can't hear enough about art and someone's love for it, but when someone gloats about being a line producer on a webseries I want to insert butt plugs in my ears. To make things as uncomfortable as possible, Hailey paused mid-sentence and revealed that she just had her period all over my bed. It was all over me too.

I don't have a problem with girls being women. I get it. It's nature and nature is only natural. It was the tone in which she acknowledged the end of my comforter and linens, "Oops, sorry," she casually shrugged, almost as if she forgot to use a coaster. I wanted to leave my own apartment and look for a new life. What had it come to?

I slept with someone I didn't like in the hopes of forgetting someone I dearly loved. It made no sense from any angle. Hailey returned from the bathroom in minutes and assumed that I wanted to hear more about her webseries. I nodded along, zoned out and paid very little attention. I just kept hearing the words, "My editor, my actors, my cinematographer." between her proud statements. Hailey made herself comfortable in my bed and I just had to fantasize about Hailey getting an emergency phone call saying that she had to leave immediately to produce her next webseries.

In my head as Hailey speedily dressed herself, I helped her lace up her boots and handed over her handbag. I was on it. There to help. Two hours later, Hailey finally realized I wasn't talkative and in a dream-like state. "Do you want me to go?" she asked. "Me? Why would you think that?" I dryly responded. "You keep looking at the TV and you're sending emails on your phone."

If only Hailey had known that the email I just sent during our 'conversation' was in fact, an email to myself saying that I hated myself and I would never ever sleep with another girl that I didn't care about. "I have to wake up early." A classic lie. And with that, Hailey gathered her things, kissed me sloppily like a second cousin and left.

I wanted to boil myself. I wasn't cut out to be an asshole despite being good at it, nor was I emotionally numb enough to "bang" girls. That's a terrible thing that men say, but I had to keep myself in check or risk turning into a douche bag permanently. The next day, Hailey sent a text--

Hey you... wanna do something ;)

Was she kidding? It was clearly a heavy flow day last night which meant, today was still a flow day. I just trashed all evidence five minutes after Hailey left at three thirty in the morning and spent all afternoon replacing sheets. I waited the appropriate thirty minutes so it was enough time for her to know my answer.

Hi Hailey, you're a wonderful girl, but I really just need to be alone. I still have feelings for my ex and it's not fair to either of us if I see you under the circumstances.

It took a full fifteen seconds for her to reply,

Are you fucking kidding me?!? I even told you that I was not a rebound right after we had sex!?! How dare you change your mind?!? Your girlfriend left you 'cos you're a psychopath! Too bad Du, because I liked fucking you and I really enjoyed talking to you about my webseries. I hope you die! FUCK YOU!

I wish I were paraphrasing, but like I said, Hailey had incredible timing. I honestly thought that she did offer rebound sex. I did make it clear that I didn't want to go out last night and my girlfriend and I just broke up. I wasn't thinking straight when I messaged, *Sure bring beer if you can.*

Was I expected to reply to, *I hope you die.* Or would any reply be proof that I was still living and disappoint? I would be insane to ask her to read the Facebook message she sent twenty four hours ago. So I didn't. I said nothing and left it at that. A week dragged on and Hailey messaged again,

Hey you, I'm in your area. Wanna grab a burger and beer?

Again, I waited the appropriate thirty minutes to

give a slight whiff of my answer and then countered,

I'm sorry, but like I said, I'm not over my ex and it's not right for me to be with anyone.

I realized that I could have phrased things better or just said nothing. Saying nothing is sometimes the smartest thing one can say. Hailey's reply back was nothing short of great literature,

You Dickhole! I sent that message to everyone on my phone. Dare you think I asked you out after you fucked me and then fucked me!?! Don't contact me ever again!

The odds that not one of those people on Hailey's phone was vegan astounded me. I also didn't understand how a successful webseries producer could only know people that lived in the Valley Village area. I feared for my life. The break up left me paranoid and believing my apartment was haunted. Now, I had someone who offered herself up sexually and then requested my death.

I moved out thirty days later and swore to never sleep with a girl that I couldn't converse with. What happened with Hailey made me feel like I had cheated on myself. Like a wise stoner friend in high school preached as he puffed away on a flimsily rolled joint, "Our bodies are like temples man. They're sacred." Okay maybe he was justifying why no girl would sleep with him, but it still counts.

3 TAYLOR

"ARE YOU LOOKING FOR A ROOMMATE?" asked Taylor, standing there in her fishnet stockings and body hugging one-piece black, mini dress. Taylor dressed like she had a thing or two to teach me in bed, but what outshined her sexual confidence was her moon-shaped innocent face and pearl necklace smile. Taylor could serve a tray of over-filled cocktails with a bigger smile than any other server at any other comedy club. Her creamy skin, cute freckles and laugh radiated a personality that could be best described as a beautiful, ripe peach. There was this warmth and fuzziness about Taylor and it was the first time I noticed her in that kind of light.

"I just got a new roommate, but I could ask around," I calmly replied. Of course in my head, I'm already thinking about Taylor walking around the kitchen in yoga pants and a sports bra. I only, for a brief moment fantasized about my current roommate committing suicide with Russian vodka and Ocean Spray Cranberry juice as a chaser. It was the preservatives in the juice that killed him.

"Okay Du, but only ask boys. I'm done living with girls, they come with too much drama and shit," Taylor snickered. "Yeah girls are stupid. Fuck them. Fuck them all." I cheered her on. Taylor giggled at the absurdity and simultaneously played with her toffee almond hair. That was enough for me to give her my secret smile. It's basically a smile I save for such occasions and works four times out of every fifteen. This happened to be one of the four.

A week of flirts on Facebook and several text messages later, I asked this newly discovered peach of a girl if she found the ideal dude roommate that wouldn't hit on her. I had no intentions of living with any girl or anyone new at this point in my life, but her plans of looking for a roommate in LA changed anyway. Taylor decided to move back to San Diego to figure out life as she put it. As an insecure comedian, constantly doubting myself I felt an instant connection. I wanted to genuinely spend time with her, not for any selfish or sexual reasons, but to simply converse as we had over the countless text messages.

They were silly conversations without purpose. On colors, on art and how we both agreed that a smell could tell a better story than a picture. "Why did I just start getting to know you, right as I'm about to leave?" asked Taylor in a dampened tone. I didn't know what to say. Nobody knows why things are the way they are. They just are. We stayed in touch and that was that. Conversations in the moment with no goal besides the moment at that very moment. A month later, a text from Taylor changed it all,

Ima comin to your hood next weekend for an event. Drinks?

It took me negative seconds to type my answer and then a moment to realize that I had to wait seven minutes before I could casually hit send on the most casual message I could think of,

Sure, msg me when ur here n we'll figure it out.

Taylor's text back was filled with excitement and appeared almost suddenly,

Nice! I'm also hanging with the girls from the club

This would be the perfect time to let you know that Taylor was of course, no longer serving drinks at the comedy club where we first met. However, and this is where it gets complicated. Taylor's friends at the club and my ex (whom I once lived with) all worked at the same club. I don't think Taylor knew that the bartender who once filled her drinks was the same girl that knew me on a deep level and hated my guts for loving too hard. Of course Taylor knew about us. Did she? Didn't girls pushing thirty get together and talk about me secretly behind my back? Of course she knew.

Then again, there's no one more closed who likes the word 'boundaries' more than my ex. Did it really matter? I mean, it's not like Taylor and I made an appointment to have sex. It was just drinks. What type of narcissist would think drinks with a girl that he's been texting for a month would lead to fornication? I didn't have answers, only questions. The only thing I was sure of was I just didn't feel right and even though Taylor and my ex weren't friends, they had friends in common. How could I allow Taylor to anticipate drinks (with or without sex) without knowing that one of her friends was currently the roommate and co-worker of an ex-girlfriend? Take that Carrie Bradshaw. Men can have drama and conflict that make little sense too.

Two days before Taylor arrives in LA, we're on the phone. She's laughing as I analyze how ducks should be offended by any aging trophy wife for stealing their look. I could tell by the sound of Taylor's sigh, that there was sexual energy exuding from her voice that particular evening. I had to tell Taylor or at least ask if she knew.

"How close are you with K*****, or her roommate K*****?" (Yes, both their names start with the letter 'K'.)

"We're all friends, I guess we're close, why do you ask?" replied Taylor. I had to let her know. I also had to let her know that it had nothing to do with the price of fish. I didn't want to be the douchebag who slept with an ex's friend's friend, but then again that's exactly what a douchebag would say. I let her know, "K***** and I used to date each other."

"Can I call you back?" she strangely asked a second after my confession. "Sure, are you okay?" "Yeah I'm fine, I just need to do something. I'll call you back in a few." A few minutes later Taylor rang, "So I spoke to K**** and told her that we had been speaking intimately and that I didn't know till just now that you and Du had been living together. I offered to not go out for drinks with you, but she said it's alright and that I have her blessing. I guess that means we're going for drinks Du."

My first reaction was, "Why did my ex get biblical and give Taylor a blessing?" My second reaction was, "This girl is fearless." My third reaction was, "I'm totally getting laid, conjugal visit style."

Now, whenever I feel sexy and unstoppable, the universe has a way of reminding me that there's no room in life for an ego. Sure enough, less than a day later I receive a text message,

I don't feel right about this Du. But if you still wanna get drinks as friends, we can.

Now, whenever the universe reminds me there's no

room in life for ego, that's when I like to test the universe back because I know we all have control over our own destinies. Just watch The Matrix if you don't believe me. I texted back,

Of course I'd still like to. Taylor, I get off just by talking to you. Well not off-off, but you know what I mean.

In my twisted man-mind, I'm thinking I called her bluff and passed with flying colors. In my heart of hearts though, I didn't want us doing anything that didn't feel right. I enjoyed talking to Taylor and the only problem, in this case was, I found her physically very alluring. We both also felt more like ourselves around each other.

Taylor and I made plans to hang out on Sunday, which meant I would manscape on Friday. Just so it's not obvious that I was prepared, in the unlikely event that something did happen. I was thinking for both parties involved really.

Taylor's presence arrived on Friday evening and my ego wasn't expecting a call till Saturday afternoon. This worked for me because I had the sniffles on Friday and my plan was to kick my cold on Saturday before our Sunday together. The obstacles and planning were piling up. When did getting laid turn into a part time job? I didn't want to send her back with a cold. Just some fond memories of my kind face.

It's Friday night and I'm in bed sipping peppermint tea and spoonfuls of honey. The plan was to nurse myself into gigilo fitness. Why was I nervous? Damn, maybe being a gentleman would attract the right girl. I didn't have to play games and was honest with Taylor from the beginning. I ordered myself to shut up. Nothing mattered. With 'Peach' as I called her now, I just didn't want to miss out on how amazing a time we would have. Best case scenario, Sunday would be drinks, conversation and wonderful sex. Worst case, I'd still have drinks and a conversation with a wonderful girl. This was a win-win situation no matter how anyone looked at it.

So midnight comes around on Friday and I'm playing nurse with myself. I get a text message from Taylor and she's had enough of hanging with the girls and wants to do something now. Most places were closing in about an hour so I asked Taylor if she wanted to come over. I realize I just manscaped today and still had a cold, but what was I supposed to do? Say, 'no' and risk offending her?

Fifteen minutes later, I waited outside my apartment building for her arrival. I slowly smoked a cigarette as Taylor parked and exited her burgundy Scion hatchback. I took her in from head-to-toe. Those high heels with leather straps hugged her feet, her toe cleavage exposed themselves, her perfectly fitting blue H & M jeans popped against her see-through white blouse with a leopard print bra underneath. Taylor dressed simply and proudly, but it was her beaming smile that made me forget about the full moon in the background. She nervously giggled as she approached me. Although Taylor walked toward me with authority, I could tell she was nervous. I smiled back and I think it relaxed her. I didn't have any alcohol to offer, but right there outside my apartment, I showed Taylor my car key and mentioned the nearest CVS was three blocks away. Only to be a good host of course, I had plans to respect the plan of 'drinks as just friends.' She declined. Wait a minute, but if she was removing alcohol from the equation, then this meant that she was also removing 'friends' from the equation. Oh girls and their mixed signals that I always seem to imagine. Again, I really didn't care about sex. Part of me didn't want sex because of the sniffles and I didn't want Taylor to fall sick.

I showed Taylor into my bedroom and asked specifically if she wanted some peppermint tea. "Yes!" She replied as if it were on her mind the entire day. I clicked on Pandora on my computer, selected 'The Xx' station and left Taylor alone in my bedroom, almost trusting her to judge me by my room. As I watched the water boil in the kitchen, I thought about what Taylor was currently thinking about.

"Does Du watch his Rambo DVD box set frequently, or did he leave it out just to impress me?" "Why does one wall of Du's bedroom look like he's planning an escape?" "These fifteen pages of paper taped randomly with flow charts don't make any sense." Yes, my bedroom did and still does come across like a crazy person sleeps there. The boiling water for the peppermint tea was ready.

In the kitchen away from Taylor (who was still in my room), I slowly poured the water onto the peppermint tea bag. I still worried about us making out and/or having sex and then Taylor waking up with a cold. That would be so mean. There was Vitamin C powder on my refrigerator and I so badly wanted to put a tiny pinch of it in her tea to keep her healthy. But then I thought of the worst case scenario, if Taylor walked in on me in the kitchen adding a suspicious white powder to her tea, she'd immediately call the cops and I'd have to explain that it was only Trader Joe's Vitamin C and I worried for her health in the unlikely event we had sex tonight. I therefore, did not add any Vitamin C because the cons of the worse-worst case scenario highly outweighed the pros of the best-worst case scenario.

Back in my room, I handed Taylor a pint size glass of Peppermint tea with two hands. It was overwhelmingly masculine with a boat load of sensitivity. It made her happy to see such a large glass, or perhaps it was my double handed Japanese style of serving tea. Either way, I was happy we weren't drinking anything with alcohol.

I asked her how the night had treated her. Taylor's sigh told me that she had enough of LA and girl drama. I'm pretty sure she felt safer and more relaxed in my bedroom, despite my bedroom walls looking the way they do.

Taylor and I spoke about life for a solid hour. It wasn't gossip, nor a pissing contest like some of you girls think we enjoy. I hate to say this, but many of you girls try to turn a wonderful date into a pissing contest. Yes, I know you're a career-driven girl, but we are not equals and will never be. I'm only too happy to learn from you and find it highly annoying when you tell me that your friends think you're funny. So what if I'm a comedian, why would I look for something in you that I already have myself. Taylor was nothing like this. There was nothing competitive about her and that made her stunningly beautiful, vulnerable and genuinely strong all at the same time. Through the art of dialog, I think Taylor and I reached an intimacy that only teenagers did back in the early 90s. The Clinton days, a simpler time for everyone. Taylor and I lay comfortably on my bed. Her eyes were glassy and I could tell by the way Taylor caressed her own face and hair, that she wanted a kiss. I knew our intimacy started brewing via text messages, so right there in front of Taylor, I texted her,

Wanna make out?

Taylor laughed furiously and hid her blushing face with her left hand and coyly texted back,

*Does that line work for you every time? ☺ *

"We'll see," I replied in speaking words, pulled Taylor in and kissed her. I could feel her smiling through the kiss.

It was dorky and sexy at the same time. Almost like a soundtrack from a Wes Anderson movie. She still didn't know about my cold and I kind of stressed out about it. Eh, screw it. It's too late now and this felt too perfect too let a little cold get in the way.

Making out and petting each other felt very real. It was almost as if we both knew each other's favorite erogenous zones. There was clear focus in her hazel-green eyes. I deeply liked that about her. There was no doubt, no fear in this girl. "I think we should slow down. I don't want to give you the wrong idea," Taylor said. "Yeah, you're right," I replied as I ignored her and continued kissing her neck and biting her ear. Taylor and I were naked in minutes.

I can't take all the credit for this, because Taylor made me want this night to last into the morning. We had poetic sex for two and half hours. I wanted to spend more time between her thighs tasting from Taylor's flower, but neither of us could resist. "You're so, sexy," Taylor said with one eyebrow raised and her head leaning back. She wasn't expecting 'sexy' from me. I wasn't either. We paced our bodies perfectly like a hit band performing live in concert. I should also add it ended with one of my biggest orgasms I've ever had. A guy usually cums, makes a face and that's that. Tonight though, I came like a bridesmaid on her frenemy's wedding night. I can't speak for Taylor, but I'm going to guess she had three or four orgasms. Maybe even five.

We lay in bed and couldn't stop talking. This time, with an even deeper comfort. I smoked my cigarette and Taylor, despite not being a smoker, borrowed it and took a tiny drag to feel close. The sun starting to rise. The poor girl only had an hour to sleep before she would have to leave for work on a one-day, all-day event. Taylor asked, "Mind if pass out for an hour?" I replied, "Of course you can," and then offered her two T-shirts to choose from. As we lay there curled up on our sides, face-to-face, Taylor's voice started to trail off. I recall her last words that night were, "Du, I don't want to fall asleep, I just really like talking to you—" and then her pretty eyes closed. A part of me wanted to kiss her, but come on, this was a first date.

I closed my eyes and heard something immediately. An hour had flown by and Taylor was putting on her clothes to leave, "Thank you for a wonderful evening." I was too tired to respond, but remembered her kneeling on the floor beside my bed to kiss me four times on the cheek. I smiled. Four. That's how many orgasms. "I'll let you know when I'm done with work," Taylor added.

"Oh wait..." I stopped her. "Please get some Vitamin water with Vitamin C or something, I might have had a little bit of a cold." Taylor chuckled, "Silly man, I'll be fine." She kissed me again. Five orgasms.

Taylor never did catch my cold. She still lives hundreds of miles away in San Diego, but with a boyfriend now. The guy is not as handsome as I am.

4 JESSICA

WHAT IF "ROMANCE" was fiction and sex was the only thing tangible? Maybe love wasn't real and the Disney movies were just exploiting an illusion. Jessica, or Jess entered my living room with a collection of porn stuffed under her arm. She then laid the DVDs across the couch with the same casualness as a Frenchman offering his mother a cigarette. I have never collected porn in my life so any collection would have seemed like a wide spread.

"I just brought whatever I could find laying around." said Jess in a lowered voice. Jess, the brunette with bangs and on anti-depressants was an interesting one. She was a retired dominatrix in her late twenties. There was a quiet sadness in her eyes, but her smile was genuine and her butt was close to perfect. Firm and tight, almost as if she were a pilates instructor. Her tits weren't big or even medium-sized for that matter, but Jess had more sexual confidence than any LA bimbo with implants. Her years as a dominatrix meant that she had seen more sexually than I could ever imagine. Her story of shoving stiletto heels up a client's ass was more information than I ever needed. I was a young, passionate man with simple needs in bed, content with doing the basics very well, if I might add. Jess however, saw the bedroom as a circus. We somehow negotiated and I guess turned it into a playground.

I didn't understand the need for props. "God gave us genitals, why bring anything else in to the mix?" I thought to myself as Jess tied rope around my wrists. "Seriously, we have nails and teeth if the mood required that sort of stuff." Fifty Shades of Grey isn't a best seller for no reason, so I went with it. Jess knew how to tie a rope better than the script supervisor on Taken. She said sexual things during sex with a polite casualness, "May I bounce on your cock?" or, "You remind me of the guy I lost my virginity to."

There was no future here. Jess even stated she didn't believe in monogamy. I made it clear from the start though, if she did want to move on to another guy or found another guy, to please let me know because I wasn't into polygamy. Never understood it, because I don't believe we are animals without souls, plus with the STD's and all that. I understand one night stands, one month stands, but I can't comprehend multiple partners. Jess respected my one request and we continued banging for a few weeks, here and there.

I guess whenever we felt lonely or horny, which amounted to the same thing.

Jess introduced me to rope and lube, but this one time she caught me off guard by escalating the stakes. "Do you want to go to an orgy with me?" I sat there with wide eyes. I've seen Stanley Kubrick's 'Eyes Wide Shut' and despite being a great movie, it made me very uncomfortable thinking of myself as unpaid background. Jess asked again, "You know, like a date?"

I respect her courage to ask me out on a date, but the words that came out of my mouth couldn't have been more small-town-girl-like. "Ewwww. People really do that? Noooo. That's not for me..." I blushed. "Oh come on, I won't fuck anyone besides you," Jess said convincingly.

"Yeah, 'cos that's what I'm worried about." I continued, "Look, I can't have sex with people watching, nor can I have sex with people having sex right in front of me. That's the weirdest thing ever. Please stop asking," I replied, almost laughing and crying on the inside. Jess respectfully let it go. I do believe sex should have an element of play, but when one keeps topping their action scenes, they're eventually going to end up with a Transformers 2.

A few days later, Jess and I both realized we weren't right for each other, even for casual smashing, no matter how good it was. I do respect and care for Jess. If she wanted,

Jess would probably seduce me quite easily with her sexual-ness. Then again, maybe not. My favorite movie is 'The Graduate' and I'm just not into Michael Bay.

5 EMMY

"I DON'T KNOW HOW you're still single Du," whispered Brittany as we both smoked our cigarettes outside a comedy club. "I don't know either," I replied loudly. I had just gotten off stage and did a decent enough job for Brittany to give me what she thought was a compliment. I mean why bring up the fact that I'm a catch if you're not going to do anything about it.

Brittany then leaned in close and stated, "I bet any one of my friends would do you." She then subtly gestured at her friends' table through the window and said, "Seriously, tell me which one you like." I have never been offered a table of girls to choose from. It was strange, almost like I were some movie star's ugly best friend. "I know you're a nice guy Du and a hopeless romantic at heart, otherwise I wouldn't have said anything like this to you," Brittany added. "I know.

I know. Of course I'm a good guy," I reminded myself and her. "So which one?" Brittany encouraged.

Did Brittany tell her friends that she'd hook them up with a comic? Is that how Brittany convinced her friends to come out and see her? Did it matter? I looked over and the one girl who I noticed from on-stage caught my attention again. I didn't want to say anything to Brittany in a hurry, so I played it cool, "You're being silly Brittany, your friends are much too pretty, just like you." I knew what I was doing.

Emmy's smile lit up not just her face, but the faces around it. She had a dancer's body and her striking features consisted of curly bright red hair, emerald green cat-like eyes and a charmingly sharp nose. This was a girl crafted for live musical theater. I nudged Brittany and said, "That girl's adorable, but I'm sure she has a boyfriend. Forget I said anything." Brittany, with her Italian zest grabbed my forearm and said, "I'll make it happen."

Later that night, I reached my apartment at 2 a.m, only to find a Facebook message from Emmy asking me out for drinks. Brittany had game. I was seriously impressed. Now if only my literary manager were as effective as Brittany, JK Rowling would be proof reading my next book. I thanked Emmy for her invitation and we decided to grab a drink at the Farmer's Market on 3rd and Fairfax.

Emmy arrived on time and greeted me with a hug under the giant clock. There was excitement in her strut, almost a dance as we walked. Her body language, physique and bounce were almost identical to Sarah Jessica Parker's character in LA Story. Emmy was more grounded with the world though. I asked if she did live theater and Emmy was surprised that I nailed it. Between her gigs as a waitress, Emmy would come to life at one of her many upcoming plays around the city. There was talent and beauty right in front of me. Our conversation consisted of mainly musicals and movies. It was light hearted, but fueled by personal stories of passion and embarrassment. Time had buzzed by and I had a show to do at a lesbian bar known as The Palms in West Hollywood. Lesbians were the best audience if you wanted to work very hard to get mild chuckles.

I politely tell Emmy that I would have loved to stay longer, but I had to be at the show two miles away. I could sense that her night was wide open so I asked her to join me, but added that I'd probably be doing the same material that she saw a couple of nights before.

Emmy squeezed my arm and said, "Du, that doesn't matter, I'd love to come." She was very kind. Moments later, we drove our cars and parked a couple of cars away from each other on Santa Monica and La Cienega. One of LA's trendier neighborhoods thanks to the gays. They just know how to do things right.

I entered and was warmly welcomed by many

friends and familiar faces. Of course, I knew majority of the comedians because we do shows together. The bartender was happy to see me too, calling out my name. I'm not a big shot. I used to volunteer as the sound guy at the same venue for shows when I first started out. This is still the easiest way to get stage time in LA and the perfect way to learn from watching. Nevertheless, I could tell Emmy appreciated being the girl beside me and walking in without paying the cover and getting served immediately at the bar before anyone around us. It's really the little things that make a date.

Twenty minutes later, the show was cancelled for lack of attendance. There was a total of one audience, Emmy. This was becoming a ritual for the venue, but to be fair, it was a Tuesday night and if I remember correctly, the show was put together at the last minute. Emmy and I decided to have another beer. I got the feeling that she thought I was a big comedian by the way she was looking at me. I reinstated that I wasn't a national touring headliner and really just a baby compared to the comedians on TV. Emmy cleverly added, "Aha, but you are the only comedian with someone here to see them tonight." Ah shucks, she was charming.

There was indeed a 1950s charm about this girl and later outside Emmy's Silver Corolla, I kissed her like Clark Gable would kiss one of his leading ladies. As I pulled away from a swooning Emmy, her eyes were still closed. It felt a little strange, so I kissed her some more to let her know the kiss was over. Then, Emmy unlocked her car, turned around to check me out and squinted her eyes at me. I waved back like a dork. Then, on the curb of LA's gayborhood, I adjusted my boner and safely drove myself home.

To be honest, I didn't feel right being with Emmy. She was so kind to me. Did I deserve this? It didn't feel right. But this girl with her theater background, had charm and genuine confidence and I did adore her company and sexuality. I was also a sucker for that nose and bright red hair that would rob the attention from any Princess blonde in her vicinity.

So I sucked it up and we planned to grab coffee around the corner near my place. It was the afternoon and I purposely asked for the afternoon so I could spend more talking-time with Emmy. I wanted to know for sure how I felt before anything physical could happen. It was coffee too, so like, nothing ever happens over a coffee.

Coffee was coffee outside the coffee shop, but also outside the gourmet ice cream place on Laurel Canyon and Ventura Blvd. It was overwhelming in a way that I can't explain too well. We both didn't want ice cream, but we craved it. Perhaps the swooning couples sharing their ice cream was enough indulgence for the two of us. Well, almost enough. Whatever craving built up from ice cream watching, we satisfied physically at my place.

Afternoon sex without alcohol was incredible. It was just as intimate as it was a work out. From the sexual heat and my constant biting, Emmy's breasts and neck were covered in red marks. I'm not going to say writers and actors are better people than bankers and lawyers, but they will always be better at sex and also better people. If you're a banker or a lawyer, I'm sorry, but you'll never have sex the way we do.

I could feel Emmy about to climax, so I pinned her down and entered her as deep as I could. We held each other like two Olympic dancers preparing for our final dismount. The back of her head dug inside the pillow, her curly red hair splayed across the bed and minutes later, she let out a scream and clawed her nails across my back. The silence after two people orgasm together is usually deafening to me. This moment however, I could hear 'The Dark Knight' playing on my TV. I think it was around the time Harvey Dent and Rachel were both waiting to be saved and they both kinda got fucked. I walked Emmy to her car and there was much arm grabbing from her end. It wasn't a cold night and the summer sun was still setting.

My problem wasn't that she felt like holding my arm. I don't know for sure. At that moment, problem was we were walking where my girlfriend and I once walked her little dogs together. One was a long-haired Chihuahua and the other was a pug. I had a soft spot for the Chihuahua, his little face would rub against my hand whenever he wanted to be petted. I felt like

I was cheating on my ex despite being single for months. I formally kissed Emmy outside her car and felt like I had just told a big fat lie.

A few days went by and I didn't know how to tell Emmy that I was a coward for taking her to coffee and an even bigger coward and asshole for sleeping with her. Surely, she must have known that I was still in pain. The act that she had seen me perform on stage was all about getting over my ex-girlfriend. Then again, jokes were just jokes to many people. Emmy asked if I was doing anything on Friday night. I had a show and realized that I should probably let her know and not waste any more of her time. I invited her and she obliged.

Now, before Emmy arrived, I texted her and warned her that there was a chance I would bomb because I had the urge to do new material that I wasn't sure of. If you think that sounds cowardly, wait till this next part. On the show, I purposely did more jokes about my ex, letting the audience as well as Emmy know that I was still hurting. The night ended and Emmy asked me, "Are you still in love with your ex?" I couldn't lie and nor did she deserve any asshole mistreating her, so I stalled instead. "Why would you ask me that question?" Emmy looked at me with her honest eyes. I had to answer, "I do... But I've moved on and that's all that matters." Emmy excused herself to use the ladies room. I knew I was the biggest asshole currently in Los Angeles and mistreated one of the nicest girl's in the world. Emmy returned and seemed fine. Maybe I wasn't an asshole. Perhaps she was just using me for sex or free comedy shows. I walked her to her car and she hugged me goodbye. "Take care Du." she said under her breath. I didn't deserve a kiss. I closed her car door on her and the sound of the ignition firing up was the sound of Emmy and I coming to an end.

A month later, I called Emmy and apologized for not getting my shit together before asking her out. She was gracious enough to accept it and tell me that I wasn't an asshole because my apology was genuine. Her words, not mine and that was that with Emmy. Today I realize it had nothing to do with feelings for my ex. Deep inside and back then, I believed I didn't deserve a girl as genuinely kind as Emmy.

6 KAYA

WHAT HAPPENS WHEN YOU MEET a version of the same you in the opposite gender of somebody else?

The Elephant Bar boasts an extremely long bar. I can only imagine the architect tried his best to match the length of the bar with that of an elephant's trunk. The patrons must have missed this detail because to compensate, there were last minute elephant-head shaped door knobs wherever the decorator could find a spot. Like many restaurants that tried too hard, the establishment didn't know what cuisine it was serving. 'Eclectic' I guess if they wanted to be cool and confused at the same time. The bar's menu consisted of sashimi, jalapeno nachos, Malaysian chicken satay and other things which I couldn't be bothered to read after I read nachos under sashimi. "I'm starving, but I don't think they have anything for me," Kaya announced.

"What do you mean? It looks like they serve everything on the menu except elephant. No wait, it's here, under gluten free," I replied. Kaya laughed, "You didn't know I was vegan?" "Really? But you seem so normal," I volleyed. "Are you Buddhist or something?" I joked. "Yes," she replied. "And I take it very seriously." My face winced internally.

The non-meat problem aside, I have to admit Kaya knew how to sit at a bar. There wasn't a man or woman who didn't pass by that didn't turn their head twice. Kaya was strikingly beautiful. She's modeled for brands including Nike and even had a role in the smash hit, Sharknado. Part German, part French, part Japanese, I guess one could say she was as eclectic as the menu, but classy, genuine and sexy as fuck. Kaya drank her whiskey neat, smoked like a French model, knew how to hold a conversation and was a single mom. This was a girl that would be on the cover of a woman magazine if those cunty editors knew what they were doing.

I nursed my Newcastle because earlier that evening, I had two drinks with the head of development from a TV network at the very same bar. I'm not bragging here, just setting shit up. The gentleman had seen me perform and asked me to hit him up for a drinks meeting. It was a fine meeting. Long story short, he was fired from the network later that week and there was no second meeting. I'm only bringing this up to illustrate that I carried the same confidence to the date from a "power" meeting that just happened an hour ago.

I listened to Kaya, really listened. She was a genuine artist throwing caution to the wind to find her true inner self. Kaya didn't apologize for being a single mom, model, actress and even slam poet. The slam poet would have been a red flag on any other night, but why look for any flags when you're sitting with the most beautiful girl at the bar. Our knowledge for the underground arts instantly connected us. I made sure drinks at the bar were over by 11:30 pm. I just couldn't be at the same bar any longer. I could sense that Kaya didn't want to go home yet. These were not spidey senses, but the fact that she said, "I don't want to go home yet." I wasn't sure if this meant my place. I named all the bad movies that were currently running in the theaters. No one in their right mind would want to see a shitty movie with midnight approaching. It was a trick question that worked. Kaya gently squeezed my boyish bicep. "Or, we can watch a movie at your place instead?" she quietly answered with a question. This was after all, a first date and I didn't want to come across un-gentleman like.

I walked Kaya to her car where she apologized for the mess at the back seat. I told her not to apologize, I wasn't planning on spending the night there. There was a shared laugh and a comfortable silence. I held the side of her waist and we kissed gloriously. It was like the center spread of an Italian fashion magazine. In her beat up mom's Nissan, Kaya followed my car to my place. I popped open a beer and we started scanning my DVD collection for a movie we both knew we weren't going to watch. Still, we pretended to care and put on Problem Child 2. We didn't get to the movie's first scene and we were already all over each other. The girl had animal-like sexual moves, yet was as graceful as a ballerina. She was a smoking hot vixen. Someone you could see on TV, pulling off a heist on a one-hour drama and then killing her boss who set up the job in the resolution scene.

Twenty minutes later, I was inside Kaya and we held each other for a very comfortable long moment. Almost savoring what was about to happen. Kaya and I were both generous with our mouths during foreplay. I explored all of her well photographed body. Her eyes squinted at me almost suggesting that she wanted it rougher. I started to bite and suck her neck and then made my way to her breasts. That's when things took a turn. My tongue sampled what could only be described as a warm, sweet liquid. My face recoiled and cringed. I wasn't sure what had just happened. I repeated the same move to be sure that it did in fact happen. I recoiled again. Kaya grabbed my face and caressed it, "Um, not to freak you out, but I'm still lactating."

My eyes widened and I put on my best Oscar face. The reality of her being a single mother hit me. Earlier that night, I didn't see how this could be a problem. So what if she was a mother? Now all I could think of was, "What if her kid was hungry?"

Of course my erection and I responded casually as ever, "Nah, that's cool." I hid my amateur poker face by nuzzling into Kaya's neck safely away from her filled breasts.

Kaya and I continued pleasuring each other like debut actors on Cinemax satisfying each other after work. "Oh Du." She called out my name multiple times as she rotated her own tits. I helped her out in that department too, but was being very careful because I didn't want to waste any smoothie. As I changed positions on her, I knocked over the beer bottle on the nightstand. Then, as the last few sips of beer spilled across my bedroom floor, Kaya climbed on top and rode me with the intensity of a Russian widow making love to her dead husband's twin brother. In return, I held her down and fucked her hard enough to forget about life.

Kaya and I lay sprawled across my bed, smoking cigarettes and sharing the ashtray that rested on my chest. Our conversation at the Elephant bar was light-hearted and casual, the complete opposite of the style of sex we just shared. There were many things we didn't know about each other, but one thing for certain, we both had seen too much of life for two kids pushing thirty.

I gently asked her how old her son was. "Three," she gingerly responded. "That's cute," I replied. It didn't bother me at all that she was a mother. It almost made her sexier. "Perhaps there was scope for a real relationship," I thought to myself. "I'm a member of Cop Watch," Kaya randomly injected as she exhaled smoke.

Here we go, I let her see me naked and she's about to invite me to her improv show. "What's Cop Watch?" I nervously asked. Kaya then proceeded to tell me how LA's police were oppressing minorities and how the Government distracted us using the media. "So wait, you watch, cops? Cops?" I asked twice. "Yeah. Someone's gotta watch them," Kaya fielded, blowing out a smoke ring. "You can google my name and read articles on my arrests," she stated.

This was very strange to me. I understand there are stories of police brutality out there, but in my personal opinion, the police have always reciprocated decent manners with decent manners. I have seen 'Serpico', but that was New York in the 70s. I'm not a fan of meter maids, but I'm not about to start following them around town with cameras.

Kaya began to speak aggressively of stories involving police brutality. She used big words, outside my vocabulary range, which meant these were the ideas and movements on various blogs written by 35 year old men who lived in their mothers' basements. I don't believe cops are bad and will always look at them as the good guys. I do, however, believe there is evil in this world, but talking about the evil is the same as spreading fear which is nothing less than handling the Devil's PR. I don't watch the news for this reason above all. I've seen and encountered enough evil. I could relate to the oppression Kaya spoke of. It hit a nerve, but I rather not worry about that and move forward with my days. I've spoken to Batman about these ideas, but sadly, he is a fictional character and our conversation never happened.

Kaya wore herself out lecturing me. I understood her ides, but I couldn't understand why someone so beautiful and talented would exhaust themselves with such a cause.

Kaya moved out of LA a month later. I'm happy to know that she's currently dating a normal guy who probably wears an argyle sweater every day. I know Kaya's had a hard life and I won't get into details, but if anyone deserves less drama, it's her. We're still friends and speak every once in a while over text. Kaya says we don't hang in person because we can't keep our hands off each other. I agree with her. I guess it's got a little to do with our eyes witnessing too much pain and we don't need to see that recognizable pain in another person. Sadly, it just makes us both horny.

7 ALEX

EVERY GIRL DOES AND SHOULD have the right to say 'no' to sex no matter what the situation. They have the power to put a stop to the act of sex, if and whenever they feel something isn't right. I just don't know why, as a guy, I don't have this same luxury.

It was a Friday night in Pasadena, after a comedy show. I enjoyed my set and this happens very rarely, but tonight I decided to reward myself and join other comedian friends and several audience members for a beer at the bar across the street. Happy patrons guzzled down beers. Some of them were swallowing sliders to coat their tummies with grease. Our high table consisted of six such individuals and the girl sitting next to me was Alex. Alex was a former navy officer who constantly played with her short, French-girl hairstyle. Her arms were delicate, but covered in sleeves of tattoos as a warning sign. Besides the intense eye contact coming from Alex's gaze, there was body contact under the table from her hands and legs. I didn't want to offend her, nor did I mind the contact so I just ran with it.

An hour later, the couple who drove her decided to head home. Customers trickled out and I politely offered to drive Alex home if she wanted another beer. Those penetrating eyes lit up. I knew I was in, but I didn't know how I felt about having sex with a friend's roommate. I knew there was no relationship here, but I just felt lonely. I didn't let it get to me. I nursed half a beer because I was driving. Our conversation sadly and mainly consisted of me, not believing in myself from time to time.

I did deliver a good set that night, but every now and then I'll doubt myself and my life's choices. Alex though, wasn't having any of it. A moment later, I felt her hand grasp the back of my neck and yank me toward her open mouth. In less than a second, Alex's garlicky tongue was inside my mouth wrestling with whatever frightened tongue it could find. I thought to myself, "When did the club start serving garlic fries?" I was barely there for the kiss. Ten minutes later, I drove us back to my place. I guess I wanted to thank her for not letting me doubt my art. That and the lonely shit.

I turned on the TV and let Pandora on Roku play whatever it was last on. It was the Amy Winehouse station and the room didn't know what to make of it. Alex sized up my bed, which that night consisted of a mattress and a disassembled Ikea bed frame resting beside it. I just didn't have the desire to put it together after moving. I really didn't care and actually quite enjoyed the TV viewing position from the ground. It was very zen-like to me. If anyone wants an Ikea bedframe, they can have it for forty bucks.

Alex, then, without any thought, started to undress herself. I thought to myself, "Does this mean we're a married couple from the fifties?" I mean, it's only polite to take off the other person's clothes and let them decide if they want to take off yours. My thoughts to myself were then cut off by something Alex said that I'll never forget.

I will admit and say with all humility that I've had a knack for attracting girls who are more attractive than me. Tonight, however was the night I realized, many of those girls, if not all, are mostly unstable. Alex leaned in, in her nakedness, lowered her voice and quietly said, "I've been feeling a lot better since I've been off my medication and I just want to thank you for trusting me." The locked door was behind her, which meant, I would have to run though her, or jump out of my bedroom window. I didn't like either of the options, so I just gave her a nervous smile instead. I noticed her left eye twitching and knew I was getting laid whether I wanted to or not. I couldn't say "no" at this point. This was a naked unstable girl. In my head, all I was thinking was, "If I back out now, she'll think it's her naked body, not because she's crazy."

The sex was awkward and bumpy. Only two of us wanted to be there. I say two, because I'm counting the voice in her head. I lay there under a naked girl who was rocking back and forth while gazing deeply at my entire face. It was quite clear I didn't want to be there. "Do you trust me?" asked Alex. "Yes of course I do," I fired back. I tried taking control of the situation, but she wouldn't let me. Alex then randomly shushed me, "Shhhhhhhhh." I wasn't saying anything at all, so I guess the shushing was directed at my body's attempt to be on top or perhaps, to her imaginary friend that was telling her what to do to me. I just lay there convincing myself that since I had a hard-on, then this technically couldn't be man-rape.

Twenty minutes of this continued, and I was already anticipating text messages the next day. I realized that I can't give Alex the full 'Du' where she'd have a memorable night of sex for forty to fifty minutes. I had to keep it bland and finish in a relatively short amount of time, but not too short. Twenty minutes seemed like the right amount of time and my Swatch watch told me it was approaching. This was a girl nice enough to have sex with me, so I did keep my manners and asked, "Do you want to finish with me?" Of course, stupid questions deserve stupid answers. "Don't worry about me Du, I usually cum the next day.... If at all." Alex retorted as she got back to bouncing. This might have been the best back handed compliment in bed ever. For the record, I've never had any sex complaints and nor did I want any. That's the thing about being a slender man (I will not use the word skinny), but slender men have something to prove in the sack. I think it makes us work harder. Sort of like how short people usually go for world domination. Honestly, I did try giving her one but someone who already decides to never have an orgasm, will probably never have an orgasm. I didn't worry about her and just finished and then clicked on HBO.

This was her cue to leave, not cuddle. I do enjoy cuddling, but since my ex-girlfriend and I broke up, I haven't been involved in that kind of stuff. My ex was the only girl I ever cuddled with and trusted. It felt like discovering home for the first time and I didn't want to share that with anyone.

Alex smothered against me and I just wanted my old life back. A home with my ex and her two little dogs, which I somehow grew to love the second I knew I was losing them. Or maybe that life was just a poster version of life. One laser etched into my mind from the countless TV commercials from childhood. I informed Alex that I had an early morning and drove her home. It wasn't the easiest task in the world as she didn't have her house keys. Alex called my friend, her roommate and woke him up to open the door. Great, now I've got explaining to do.

I did try having sex with Alex again, but only to prove to myself that I could get a non-orgasm-having girl to turn into an orgasm-having-girl. It just didn't sit right with me that such a girl could exist. She declined seeing each other for sex. I guess I'm not as sexy as I thought.

8 PENELOPE

"WHAT ABOUT PENELOPE?" a common friend of ours whispered quietly. Great, I was turning into one of those fucking people where friends thought they had to start playing matchmaker. "What about her?" I responded. I never looked at Penelope as a possibility or even as a girl for that matter. I guess it's 'cos I met her when I was happily in a relationship and all girls just seemed to morph into a huge collection of opposite genders that had no effect on my eyes or heart. Besides, Penelope wasn't my type. She was nice.

Penelope's hero was Oprah Winfrey and she believed in shit like vision boards and astrology. You could say she was the type of girl I laughed at in school and even made fun of for doing her homework. But... for some strange reason, over the next few weeks, Penelope and I started spending time with each other.

Penelope and I would grab a quick bite after doing an open mic together. Head to Del Taco and spend another hour there, laughing and making fun of each other. What was this? We'd kid about being famous in the near future. As a joke, one night, I sat her in the back seat of my car and chauffeured her two blocks away to our nearest Del Taco. Penelope cackled all the way there. One night, she did the same thing to me and I pretend "fired" her for putting me in her Chevy with roll down windows. I didn't know what was going on, I just knew I liked spending time with Penelope and making her laugh. I wasn't my usual miserable self either. For a happy person, I'm pretty sure she was actually happier around me too.

Did I like her? Did Penelope like me? Why was I asking myself questions like I was in the fifth grade? This is stupid. You're stupid. Oh those eyes. Why the fuck does she have to have such beautiful eyes? Ah man, her hair smells like Shampoo. That's not fair. Is Penelope wearing make-up on her cleavage to highlight her breasts? I know about that trick. Who is she trying to impress? It can't be me. I'm her comedian slash Del Taco buddy.

A week later, Penelope sends me a text asking for help with a script and offers to help me with mine. I oblige. I'm always happy to help. I didn't need help on mine. It was done. I didn't want to tell Penelope that I didn't want her notes though. It would have been mean and besides, I didn't want her to feel like she owed me anything for helping her with her script.

It was a Monday evening at Penelope's apartment in Sherman Oaks. Sherman Oaks is where people live when they can't afford Beverly Hills, but have their eyes set on it. It also happens to be a few blocks from Van Nuys, the arm pit of the valley. This wasn't the first time I had been to Penelope's. I gave her my story notes and from her smile and excitement, I think they helped. There were also a few minor typos and misspellings which she didn't seem to care about. There was a moment of shyness when Penelope announced she didn't know the difference between 'worse' and 'worst'. I have a few words that I'm not a fan of myself. I patiently explained the difference and made her feel comfortable for not knowing everything. Penelope then asked if I wanted to drink some wine with her.

At this point, for the record, I did not have any clear feelings for Penelope. I respected her as a friend and that was all. I don't, however, like it when girls need to consume alcohol to get physical. The setting just didn't feel right. An hour went by and Penelope slipped into her pajamas and returned. I felt her leg near mine and I think I was supposed to make a move. It didn't feel right. It was getting late now and I didn't feel the moment. The thing about making the first move, with me at least, I either feel confident and can even hear a jazz song. Or if it's not right, I just feel like there's an old man beside us playing music from a boombox.

It felt like one of those boombox nights. Maybe it wasn't meant to be. Screw it, I'm going in. Then, as smoothly as I went for Penelope's face, her face, just as gracefully turned away. "Oh Du, we're friends." "Oh, yeah, I know. I was just... Yeah."

Penelope gracefully patted my thigh, "You're amazing, but we work together." I didn't have a problem with the amazing part of the statement, I did however, have a problem with the fact that she thought we worked together. "Worked together?" That really didn't make any sense to me. So I asked, "What makes you think that we work together?" "You're a comic, I'm a comic. You know," Penelope responded.

I couldn't see my expression, but I can only imagine that it appeared as if my face entered a room of bad odor. "Penelope, that doesn't make any sense. We're comics. I get that, but that's like saying, you're a bartender at TGIF, I'm a bartender at Chili's, we work together." Penelope cackled, as she does. It was sweet. Neither of us felt uncomfortable. I still should have listened to the old man playing his boombox. We hugged goodbye as friends and the night was over. No awkwardness.

Three days go by and I get a text from Penelope,

Du, are you still coming with me to the wedding?

Ah fuck, well this is awkward now. A conversation from a week ago hit me like a piano to the face. It went something like this,

Du, would you like to be my date to this wedding on Saturday the fifth? I really need someone to go with and I want to show-off. Will you be my show-off date?

Is there a cover charge? I responded.

Yes.

Penelope played along. I'm pretty sure she could have found someone else, but maybe she was re-asking not to hurt my feelings for making a move. I'm handsome on a good day and all that, but seriously, I'm in no means, a show-off date.

I didn't feel like dressing up and wearing banker pants or black leather shoes. I seriously hate dressing up and going to weddings or any event where people wear phony smiles. I always end up being better looking than the groom and then he starts giving me dirty looks. Dude, it's not my fault your douche bag brother took you tuxedo shopping and you didn't bother spending money on a hair stylist. Take a gay friend, this is your fault. I digress. What was I going to tell Penelope? I didn't want her to feel bad for rejecting me. Then again, why do something that makes me unhappy? Forget her, I needed to be fair to myself. So I replied,

Sure, as long as there's still no cover.

I could sense Penelope on the other end beaming a

smile. I didn't want to go, but the misery I would bear wouldn't compare to the happiness I could give. As a brother of two older sisters and a single mom, I completely understand what weddings mean to girls and why they get vulnerable and why they can't go alone. On the other hand, I didn't like being the guy friend that did these sort of favors. I don't know why to this today, but I chose Penelope's happiness over mine. To make things fair, I asked her to drive to my place first and then I'd drive us there in my car.

Saturday afternoon came around and I put on my black slacks, a burgundy Hugo Boss shirt and a loosely tied, skinny black tie. I kept a black sports coat handy on the chair, in case Penelope wanted me to go all out. If I was going to be miserable, I might as well look good being miserable. I couldn't find a black belt though. Okay, I didn't own a black belt. I had casual belts for jeans and shit, but didn't own a single leather belt. Like I said, I never cared enough for dressy occasions. I didn't feel comfortable at all going, but then I checked myself out in the mirror. Beast! For some reason, my hair was having a perfect day and my shirt popped against the tie which subtly rested against my man of a chest. If I had an office job today, I would get promoted just for dressing to kill. Penelope texted, she was on her way up.

I opened the door to let her in and that's when I saw Penelope, but this time for the very first time. She awkwardly marched up in a hurry wearing her elegant burgundy cocktail dress, pink flip flops and no make-up. "I still have to get ready," Penelope stated as she dashed toward the nearest mirror with a tote bag.

I kept the compliment of her looking better without makeup to myself. Penelope gleamed naturally. As she applied her make up, I offered with or without jacket. 'Without' was the answer I nudged her toward. Fifteen minutes later Penelope was ready and then climbed up on her extremely high heels. She was still several inches lower than me and cracked a joke about it.

Penelope was now all dolled up. I once again fought back giving her a compliment because my rule has always been, one compliment per evening. Anything more than that, then it's just annoying or can come across artificial. Less is more is a rule I abide by. It was still bright outside, so I wore my sunglasses that might as well have been from Don Draper's dresser. Between my perfect hair day and shades, I'm quite surprised Penelope didn't pay me a compliment. Or maybe she did, but I was too busy listening to the voices in my head on why the fuck I was going to this shindig in the first place. I opened my car passenger door for Penelope, let her in and we were off.

The drive was relaxing and neither of us mentioned the other night. I guess you could say it was a regular date, but without any pressure. Someone had already been turned down so neither of us had anything to gain or lose. It was just in the moment, good conversation. Much like our Del Taco dinners. Forty five minutes pass and we pull into the venue's driveway. It was an apartment complex, or so I thought. Penelope quietly uttered, "They changed the location yesterday, so it might be a little disorganized." I already felt like I was being scammed. I pull into an open spot and together, we strutted toward the entrance like two big shots. Penelope grabbed my hand and I awkwardly held it back. "You don't want to hold my hand Du? I want them to think we're dating," said Penelope. Jesus, why am I such a pussy when it comes to girls? "Sorry, here," I replied and warmly clasped her hand.

The reason I didn't feel comfortable holding Penelope's hand was because I didn't want to find out that I *liked* holding her hand and sadly, I did like holding her hand and that's what I didn't like. That makes sense right? We enter and I notice a bunch of old people aimlessly looking for something to do. That's when I realized the scam and loved it!

The wedding was being held in the ballroom, or I should say, Bingo room of an old peoples' retirement home. It was Saturday night. Their favorite night of the week and we had taken over their night club. I felt terrible for them, but it was just too hilarious for me feel bad. Penelope and I made our way in and I couldn't stop laughing on the inside. "Act like you're my boyfriend," Penelope quickly added as we entered. I didn't like that she said that.

At the entrance of the Bingo room, there were name tags on chocolate balls which were arranged in the shape of the ballroom. Someone had been there all morning and was probably very proud of their wasted time. Seriously, fuck any occasion where people have to dress up this nice. Penelope nervously led the way in and like tourists, we looked for table number eight. I could tell Penelope wasn't relaxed yet. I told her not to worry and we'd just sit anywhere till someone told us to move. I even added that she could blame me if any asshole wanted to be an asshole. Through the maze of tables, I chose the best table in the room. It was safe from the crowded bar and even the noise of the kitchen. It also happened to be table number eight. Go figure. Penelope agreed that it was the best table and when we finally sat ourselves down, I heard her let out a huge sigh of relief just for arriving.

I put on pants, a shirt and a loosely tied neck tie. For Penelope, it was over two weeks of panic, hours of getting ready, hair care the night before and a three minute walk in five inch heels which must have felt like a mile and a half. I understand why girls put so much pressure on themselves for these things and I will also say that I admire them for it. So in my kindest voice, I let her hear the truth and my one compliment, "You did it Penelope, you're the most beautiful girl in the room."

Penelope blushed and then squeezed my hand. It was all that she needed to hear. Penelope felt as beautiful on the inside as she was on the outside.

CLICK She strong armed me again with another smile into taking a selfie of the two us. "We make a good couple," Penelope stated, not I. I asked her not to tag me on Facebook. I didn't want any evidence, nor did I want any questions from anyone we commonly knew. Tonight was a one-night charade, nothing more.

Two hours flew by and we spoke about everything under the sun as we people watched. It was a stress free date because it wasn't a date. I blew my only five bucks in cash on the first tip. I wish I had more money to tip the bartender, because I felt guilty asking Penelope three times for change to tip him. It was fine though, we're technically "co-workers" after all.

On our way out before leaving, I waited outside the ladies room for Penelope. This was when an old woman approached me and asked me what was going on. I told her it was just some wedding, nothing exciting. The old woman who had been ignored by the other old people looked up at me and in the saddest of voices said, "It must be nice to be young." Just then Penelope walked out and joined us. I didn't know what to say. I wanted to tell the old woman that I wanted to trade places with her. I had enough of bullshit with dating, love, romance and sex. It was exhausting and I wanted it to be over so I could settle down. Here I was about to drive a girl back to her car which was parked outside my place. I was going to hang up my nicest shirt and hate myself for being the guy who had been pushed around by an intelligent girl with a naïve smile. Instead, I just smiled and said, "It was a pleasure talking with you ma'am." If only that old woman knew the bullet she dodged.

I drove us back to my place, but Penelope was too excited to call it a night. She asked if I wanted to go out drinking or do something, but I already had my two drinks quota for the night. I explained that I can't be drinking and driving and nor would I ask her to. I also wasn't a fan of drinking more than two drinks, driving or not. I've witnessed enough drunks in my childhood to last two lifetimes. I politely offered Penelope my place as a venue in case she wanted to have one last beer. She sat up and sang, "Yeah!" and after a quick CVS pit stop, we were at my place on my bed popping open bottles of Stella. This wasn't what I had in mind for a fake date.

The only thing worse than being rejected once, is being rejected twice. I told myself, I will not make a move on her and I did not. Like any two friends, we watched HBO and lay in my bed sipping Stellas. I felt her head and body closing in on me. I'm not going to make a move, I'm not going to make a move. Her head found my shoulder and she gingerly curled her legs making her knees fit perfectly under the pit of my knee. It felt snug, but what didn't feel snug was Penelope's friend constantly texting her. I didn't care for her friend. Whenever Penelope and I were alone, this fucking friend would somehow text like a controlling mother. I didn't know what to make of this and every two to three minutes, the phone would go off. I had enough of it distracting me from the TV. I asked Penelope, "Does someone desperately need you?" Penelope replied, "No, it's just Marcie, she's asking how tonight went."

I know a cock block when I see one, 'cos it's usually a douchebag or a douchebag girl who can't get laid themselves. The text messages were getting overwhelming and I could see that Penelope was furiously responding because her friend was being a cunt. "If you have to go, it's alright," I said. Penelope sighed, "I told her that I was drinking with you, but now she wants me to take a cab to see her at my place." I'm no city planner, but I suggested, "If your friend really wants to see you, then ask her to pick you up from here." Penelope knew I was right. There was no point taking a cab to hang with her best friend, when she was currently having a great time, almost cuddling on a fake date with a man who didn't own a leather belt.

Within ten minutes, her cunt-friend parked outside and our charade of a date came to an end. Later that night, I watched Speed with Keanu Reeves to get my mind away from things. Sadly, Sandra Bullock had the same naïve smile and the same comedic voice as Penelope. And that's when I realized, I was in trouble.

9 FRANCES

YOU COULD SAY FRANCES was cool on paper. She had a carefree attitude, was knowledgeable about music and called herself a documentary filmmaker on the side of her four-days-a-week-as-a-server job. There was this big-esque confidence Frances carried and her eyes were gentle, but I could tell those same eyes could turn on a dime if the moment called for it. "I'd ask if you wanted to get a drink, but I have to wake up early." Frances smoothly stated. This girl with a heart shaped butt had chops. This was a very suave way of saying, "Ask me out now and I'll say yes." I did and the date was set.

Sunday at the Blue Dog in Sherman Oaks was an ideal place for a beer. It's cute, charming and what stepped it up a notch was the infinite framed portraits of customers' dogs across every wall. I truly dug this place. It was a decent date which ended with a tender, yet wet enough kiss to get a chubby. I walked Frances to her car and as I closed her door said, "I'll call you." This should have been the end of the conversation. A polite giggle would have been nice. However, the red flag which I missed out on presented itself very subtly. Frances replied, "Yeah you will." and drove off.

I walked back to my car thinking, "Well, that was kind of arrogant." It was a first date with a kiss, not a one-night-stand where she banged my brains out. Why would she think I was surely going to call? Maybe her server position at her restaurant was a cover for some profession that held power over one's dreams. I let it slide. I know my imagination likes to wander so maybe it was just me reading into things that didn't exist. A few days later, date number two had been set. Frances and I met up at Pitfire Pizza on Lankershim and Magnolia in the NoHo arts district. This is where people pay Sunset Blvd. prices for a mediocre pizza. Whatever, it was convenient enough for where Frances was at the time and more importantly, close enough to my place in case the second date went well.

Now I'll say this, I have no problem whatsoever paying for a lady. It's just the way I was raised and like I've stated before I believe men and women will never be equal. We are the Yin and Yang and keep each other balanced. Men pay for food because we no longer hunt for it. It's that simple. The one time I lived with a girlfriend, groceries and trash were my responsibilities. If the girlfriend wanted to shop for groceries, then I'd hand her cash. It's just the way of my world. So please understand how strongly I feel about men paying for food. Frances and I order at the counter. I of course, let her place her order first. It was just a squash soup. Maybe six or seven bucks. Could have been less. I order a beer and Frances orders a red wine. The polite thing to do ladies, is the whole "Let me pretend to reach for my lady purse" act. This is where you fumble in the darkness of your handbag moving your designer money holder from one corner to the other. This is completely fine, hilarious and dating etiquette. What isn't cool was what Frances' next action was.

I take out my card and before I could blink hear, "Why thank you kind sir," as Frances cemented her hands by her sides. To make my wound burn more, I'm pretty sure Frances said the exact same thing on our first date. Hell, Frances makes more money as a server in an upscale Beverly Hills restaurant than I do as a comedian slash author slash dog sitter. I let it go.

It's fine. It's just a fucking soup I tell myself. Forget about manners man, pretend it's just another glass of wine. I was doing a terrible job convincing myself I wasn't broke. I'll spend on a girl, but ladies, a little appreciation goes a long way. No one's asking for their dick to be sucked. The handbag fumble is more than enough of a gesture. I don't even need a 'thank you'. So yeah, I let it go.

We sit down and our conversation begins. I wasn't paying full attention because I was sizing up her designer hand bag. There were so many pockets she could have chosen to play with. It would have been an incredible second date if someone had taught this girl dating etiquette. The next thing that bothered me shouldn't have. Or maybe it bothered me because of the two time scam pulled. I don't know how, but Frances managed to arrogantly eat her soup. This was soup, the most humble of dishes eaten by people across the world in every culture. How does one eat soup arrogantly? Frances had the napkin resting on her lap and brought the soup spoon to her face. There was no leaning in to enjoy its heartiness. Her ego exuded from every spoonful.

I kid you not, Frances even ate this bowl of soup without any slurping sound. The word 'soup', for the record is named after the sound that is made when one slurps. 'soup' 'soup' 'soup'. Our Neanderthal ancestors must have named it back in the day before speech was invented. Soup was meant to be slurped because it was named after slurp. An hour later, we walked to our cars and I ask, "So you wanna come over?" This is dating etiquette too. Frances checked her watch and replied, "Yeah that works." Apparently, it wasn't my charisma or great hair day that was the deciding factor, but her schedule.

Frances followed me back to my place and I showed her to my room. "I feel like I'm in a college dorm room," Frances said in a passive manner. This was getting annoying,. I better have sex with her now and I'm not going to be great at it, on purpose.

I selected a boring documentary. Frances did feel like she was in a college dorm room, so why not let her learn a little. Soon enough we start making out and I'm sucking on her boobs. There was no passion from my side. I felt like I had been judged for not having money and unappreciated for over-paying for over-priced squash soup. These were clearly my own insecurities, which I realize now. However, this was a second date and no one doubts themselves on a second date. It's judgment day. Frances and I dry humped like a hip hop video and she didn't let me take off her black tights. Her top was off though, weird. For some reason a girl topless with bottoms on, looks as appealing as a man bottomless with a shirt on. I entertained myself as I set my body in automatic make out mode. "Let's take this slow. It's not you, it's me, I'm weird," Frances said. I slowed down. I knew I wasn't getting laid. I thought to myself, "How many soups did this girl need for me to see her ass cheeks clap?"

This wasn't what I was looking for. Turns out, it wasn't what Frances was looking for either. I asked her out again via text and Frances replied,

I really admire you, but I just don't feel a connection.

Not surprised, because I wasn't into her either. I laughed to myself and replied,

I understand. Thanks for being honest. See you around.

I haven't seen Frances or eaten soup since. I do have a new dating rule though: If I see any girl eating soup as if it were invented for them, I'm staying far away. 'Arrogance' and 'Self-entitlement' is something I can't tolerate. Sadly, it's not another shade of confidence, but a deluded version of it. Confidence to me at least, is the willingness to be vulnerable, honest and feminine. Seriously, so what if my bedroom looks like a college dorm room. You're a pompous girl and you call yourself 'Edgy.'

10 PENELOPE PART TWO

COULD THIS FINAL CHAPTER be the happy ending? It's Sunday, or the very next evening after the wedding night, if you prefer. Penelope came by to pick up her car which was parked outside from the night before. She came upstairs to kill some time and for some strange reason, or because I'm a girl on the inside, I could sense her wanting to continue where we left off from the night before.

We popped opened another bottle of beer and soon enough, we were watching the same TV show (Little Britain) on HBO and she was curled up in the same position right beside me. Again, I told myself, I'm not going to make a move. But then, thirty minutes later the strangest thing happened... Our heads turned toward each other at the same time and our lips just found themselves gently kissing. It was the kiss after the longest twenty hour linger. We made ourselves comfortable and started making out. It didn't feel like our parents were in the next room because her asshole friend wasn't texting. It just felt right.

Several minutes passed and things heated up. Penelope did have a beer, but that couldn't have been the deciding factor. She had an entire day to think about whether kissing my face would be worth risking our friendship. I mean, we did see what happened to Ross and Rachel on 'Friends'. They were friends when they split up and it's not like NBC would ever lie to anyone. Penelope stopped kissing to fix her hair and climbed on top of me, "Don't get all awkward tomorrow on me Du," she insisted. "Why would I be awkward?" I replied as I pulled her toward me. I kissed her collar bone and Penelope continued breathing heavily into my ear. "Don't like write a poem about me," she added. "Hey don't flatter yourself. Let's just keep it simple." I ended the small/big talk there and we continued making out like frat sisters on a second date.

Penelope didn't let me take off her shirt or pants that night. I walked her to her car and she was leaving for New York the next day. I could tell Penelope was happy that she took the leap from friends to kissing friends. There was a certain bounce in her step and I didn't call her out on it.

From New York, Penelope began texting. She knew I had a soft spot for that city and I think she wanted to tell me about how great it was. Or, she was at a Starbucks and had no one interesting or weird enough to watch. Either way, I could safely assume she was thinking about me. Several text messages later, a picture message beeped on my phone. It was the selfie of us from the wedding from a few days ago. Penelope's message was,

Here, so you have one too.

It was sweet of her to put herself out there.

Later that night, Penelope messaged again and politely asked if I could get her from LAX airport. I thought for a long minute. It was a big decision because picking someone up from the airport will always be a grand gesture. There's a reason the climax to 90% of the romantic comedies endings are at airports or are races to the airport. It's a location where emotions run high and the stakes just get bigger. Train stations worked in black and white movies and now sadly, it's the airport.

I'll happily pick up a friend from the airport, but it has to be a close enough friend. Penelope, a week ago, I wouldn't have hesitated, but now that we were making out or whatever, there's a certain element of, "let's-not rush-into-things" syndrome because of the poem shit she said. Was I supposed to pick her up? Wasn't I coming on too strong if I said yes? Hey, she asked you man! I began my reasoning;

This is a girl that is romantically immature and indecisive. Knowing girls the way I do, the smartest thing for me to do would be to NOT pick her up and just say I was busy. That way, she'd either know how she felt and/or want me more or less. Perhaps I'm overthinking shit. I didn't want to play games. It was just a fucking ride. Then again, this was a girl and girls needed to be left alone at times to know their deepest desires. Yeah okay that's what I'll do, I'll tell her I'm busy.

Penelope lit up like a Christmas tree when I pulled to the loading curb at Terminal two. The plan was to take her straight home to say bye, but Penelope was hungry. This was a bit much I thought to myself. Maybe *she* was coming on too strong. Did it matter though? We were, after all, friends for over a year now. We both knew each other well. After dinner I helped Penelope with her suitcase to her front door. Penelope stood there awkwardly and then leaned forward. I kissed her goodnight. I let her know that I was leaving town in four days for work and we could do something before that. Penelope tip toed and kissed me again. It felt brilliantly simple.

Penelope and I scheduled ourselves to hang out at my place the night before I flew out. I'd be away from LA for ten days. This would also be our third non-date.

I was in high spirits after a decent meeting so I definitely was looking forward to "pre-airport" sex with someone I cared about. Penelope texted asking,

You wanna just come over instead?

It felt like something was wrong. The word 'just' being the danger word to me. What was changing plans about? Nah, she probably just feels more comfortable having sex in her bedroom than in mine. My bedroom was filled with clothes and an unpacked bag, papers on the ground. It was a wreck.

Sure. Running home for a bit, give me thirty

I arrived at Penelope's front door which was ajar for some reason. I thought to myself, was Penelope waiting in lingerie with flower petals leading to her bedroom? I opened the door and saw her roommate in a butch tank top and sweat pants. "Hi, I'm Sophie." Fuck, another cock block. I didn't even need sex to be honest. I just thought it would be nice to spend time with Penelope before leaving town.

Here I was instead, being scammed into babysitting her thirty year old roommate who looked thirty five and acted twenty five. Sophie, Penelope and I sat there awkwardly staring at the TV. Tim Gunn and Project Runway couldn't have been more offensive. This was mean. I could be packing or hanging out with a friend, performing on stage or watching TV at home.

Instead I was sitting with two girls as they watched some shitty reality show. I was polite and nice to Sophie, thinking she'd get the hint and leave us alone. She didn't. As soon as Project Runway ended, Sophie wanted to watch New Girl. Luckily, Penelope nor Sophie couldn't figure out how to connect their computer to the TV. I could have easily used my Hulu account and helped them, but fuck that. I sat there smoking my e-cigarette as the two girls fumbled with chords. I wanted to leave, but then of course, I'd be the rude one.

Sophie finished her chamomile tea and Penelope and I finally moved into her bedroom. We made out and I could feel Penelope not feeling it. It was like she didn't want to be there. I could sense that she didn't want me to be there either. All I'd been was nice and honest from the start, but sadly there's no bigger turn off than being available. I know this procedure didn't work on girls all my life, but this was a friend who asked me to not be awkward or different and I didn't want to either. So I flat out asked Penelope, "You seem pre-occupied... You alright?" The other two times we had made out, it felt natural, now all of a sudden, she was pulling away. Penelope replied, "I'm fine... Maybe 'cos I was drinking the other times."

This was the meanest thing Penelope could have ever said to me. In the moment to me, it meant 'I need to dull my senses in order to exchange affection with you.' Girls, you might as well falsely accuse a guy of being a date rapist if you're going to say something like that. What was the point of being open and vulnerable if the payback was usually a slap in the face? This gentleman shit was a fucking scam.

What is it about relationships where we reject kindness and welcome meanness? Does no one have any self-worth? We are all damaged children with grown-up hormones, but I just didn't have the time or the patience. This wouldn't work. Penelope cuddled. I pulled away and asked, "Why are we cuddling?" It wasn't fair that she thought she could benefit from my human warmth. I'm not a sweater, I'm a human and the alcohol comment was a disgusting thought to have and a sick thing to say to someone.

I left fifteen minutes later and said goodnight. Penelope pulled me toward her and kissed me goodnight. I felt nothing and gave nothing. Ten days later, I returned and wanted to see if I was wrong and just being an asshole complicating things for being sensitive. I really hoped to be right about being wrong. I went to the regular open mic we frequented and ran into Penelope. She said "hi" enthusiastically, then "goodnight" just as enthusiastically within the span of a Beatles song. It was over.

Apparently Penelope knew I was amazing, but not amazing enough or should I say disconnected enough to feel a connection. Over a phone conversation days later, she apologized with this rehearsed niceness that only seemed condescending. "I hope we can still be friends and it won't be awkward from now on," Penelope announced as the new meanest thing she could think of. "Yeah, that's not going to happen," I replied.

THE HAPPY ENDING

In this book's introduction, I promised you a happy ending. I did not however, say it would be mine. Maybe I'm bitter from my childhood seeing my parents hurt each other because that's all they knew. I'm also certain there was a third party involved benefiting from their inevitable split. I've even seen something similar happen with girls that I've cared for with their best friends or mothers or sisters. These outsiders plant seeds of advice only to sabotage and "protect" a girl from being in love.

Or maybe romance no longer exists and in this disposable society where TVs and cars last no longer than five years, where apps like Tinder, Lulu, websites like OKcupid, Ashley Madison, Match.com, Christian Mingle, Plentyoffish bombard us with so many options upon options, it's so much easier to walk away from a relationship than to look for, fight for and let true love blossom. As individuals, couples and even objects age, they carry stories and memories with them. Much like the old woman at the wedding or the whistling middle-aged man at the sports bar believing love will fall in his lap for being himself. For me, that is hope, that's love and as clumsy as a heart might feel, I don't think I or anyone should be keeping it in a vault or wearing a mask to advertise ourselves as somebody else.

I will never date online. It goes against everything that love stands for. To write up a two dimensional version of myself and post it online would be placing my heart in the relationship clearance bin. Then what? Hope someone will pick it up and then mistreat it for being on sale? In today's times of the media creating news and people being so cruel to celebrities just to steal quick beam from their spotlight, there's nothing more important than finding true love to distract us from the distractions.

Statistically and logically speaking, love just has to happen once and we all know we've been struck by lightning at least that many times. Either way, for the sake of your own sanity, stop looking for guidance, stop listening to Dr. Phil, to Oprah, stop looking for love online (it can only lead to porn) stop buying books on dating, unless of course, it was written by me. I did promise a happy ending, but what I didn't mention was that the happy ending was yours.

It's very simple because you know everything you already learned in kindergarten. Just take off your mask, love your freckles, wear lower heels, less make-up, slurp your soup, open your heart and be yourself. Love will find you. The connection you seek (or perhaps even avoid) is out there seeking you. Be vulnerable and it will strike you like a big, wonderful, natural disaster.

This is all coming from a dating un-expert who also believes pajamas are the best thing in the entire world. But then again, that's exactly why you can trust me.

ABOUT THE AUTHOR

Du Kirpalani was raised by a single mother and two older sisters. He currently lives in Los Angeles where he performs stand-up across comedy clubs and local bars. Early in 2013, Du showcased at the Sundance Comedy Series and has featured at the Egyptian Theater in Park City. His webseries, 'Becky: The Most Annoying Girlfriend in the World' was an official selection at the Beverly Hills Film Festival and won second place at the Burbank International Film Festival. Du's debut book, '100 Poems For My Ex & 10 Jokes For Me' is also available on Amazon.com

If you enjoyed 'Side Boobs', please leave a five star review on Amazon.com and let your friends know they should get a copy before they sell out. To stay in touch, friend Du on Facebook.com/CatchTwentyDu, Twitter.com/CatchTwentyDu or visit his blog at www.CatchTwentyDu.com

DU KIRPALANI

OTHER WORKS FROM DU

The author's debut book is available on Amazon.com

Praise for '100 Poems for My Ex & 10 Jokes for Me':

"This book comes with beautiful poetry and wonderful comedy. No author in history has dared attempt such a thing unless you count that guy Shakespeare."
– Brian Kiley, comedian and
Emmy award winning writer for CONAN

"Du Kirpalani has cracked open his chest to share the ruined spectacle of his heart. It's a bloody mess, pumping and seething and groping to reclaim lost moments of a doomed love affair. And then come the jokes, light moments forged from the darkness, and the laughter makes us sadder, but the sadness no longer seems without hope. Du shows us that every comedian is dying inside, but in every heartbreak lies the birth of a joke."
- John Carr, producer of THE BACHELOR and VANDERPUMP RULES

"When comedians write books, they can tend to fall prey to false bravado, abusing the art of acerbic humor, which might work on stage, but does not bode well on the page. Du Kirpalani's book wears no such mask. This book is full of heart; complex in its simplicity about love, loss and healing through humor. Then, just when we think he might be a stalker disguised as a poet, he zings us with a great joke, letting us know he's still sane."
– Katie Love, author of CUBICIDE

KISSES FOR YOU

How many kisses do I have for you,
A universe of kisses to the power of universe,
That's how many kisses I have for thee,
Just for your face and face alone

Here's a secret my sweet sweet girl

On our very first kiss,
I wished it were my very last kiss,
A kiss that never had to end,
That's what kissing you meant to me

To put it simply,
Kissing you was kissing you,
It made me feel like kissing you

YOUR SECRET WISH

What's that there,
An eyelash on your cheek,
It's resting there patiently,
Waiting for your wish to seek

Here it is beautiful girl,
Laying on my digit,
Make your wish now,
Make it count so much

You close your soul's windows,
Beam a smile,
And a wish you make,
Your eyes still closed,
A tiny fairy arrives

A quill she whips out,
And jots down your wish,
A font so tiny,
To fit on your crescent hair,

The wish is engraved,
A gush of wind from your lips

The mini fairy takes off,
She's up and away,

Straight to the heavens,
To grant your selfless wish

Your eyes,

They open,

Just in case,

I sweetly kiss you,

Was it,

Was it,

Your secret wish

HOW JOHNNY DEPP MADE ME BEAUTIFUL

a short story by Du Kirpalani

EVERY FOUR YEARS, the movie star Johnny Depp gives back to his fans and selects one young man to mentor. Not to be an actor, singer or canvas for tattoos, but to be 'Beautiful'. I was lucky enough to be Johnny Depp's second student. The previous man, I hear exploded from too much beauty and is now a distant planet.

It was a Tuesday morning. I arrived at his stunningly gorgeous villa. I headed towards the front door, my heart smiling like a Beverly Hills dentist. DING DONG. I rang the grandiose doorbell. Everything felt right, but there was no answer. Seven cigarettes later, I summoned the courage to ring the doorbell again. I pressed it ever so gently, as if I had any control over its volume. Thirty seven minutes later, I seriously needed to use the bathroom. This was getting a bit much. Perhaps the doorbell was being muffled by all the Handsome that was waiting for me inside.

My bladder couldn't take it anymore. I turned around to look for a plant to triumphantly piss on, and there he was… Johnny Depp. He had been standing behind me in all his beauty the entire time. Now I'm not a man into men, however Johnny Depp is a classic beauty. If Johnny was a car, he'd make other cars feel beautiful just for driving in the lane beside him. His angelic face stared right though my soul and then in his poetic deep voice he uttered, "Are you going to urinate in my garden?" I responded, "Of course not Mr. Depp." But I hadn't peed in hours and I just drank an entire bottle of Smart Water. Those skinny bottles can be deceiving. Johnny curved a blessing smile and replied, "I'm not letting you inside just yet." he continued, "From true vulnerability, beauty is born."

I didn't understand what this had to do with my peeing. Johnny then placed his hand on my shoulder and silently said, "Pssssssssssss." Two seconds later, my bladder let loose. As the warm urine leaked through my socks, Johnny added, "A man is at his most vulnerable when he is peeing in the presence of an actor. Therefore your journey to true beauty has now begun." It made complete sense. Johnny snatched back his hand from my shoulder and then embraced me. A little pee trickled on his left boot.

Moments later, Johnny held his hand to his front door and it magically creaked open. The collection of warm colors, textures and furniture sucked me right in. It was as if gypsies and Zen monks had agreed on the same interior decorator. "Who designed this place?" I asked. "Never mind that my friend, how about taking a shower before your wee-wee begins to create a fowl stench." Johnny then flipped his perfect hair and directed me to the nearest bathroom. Twenty minutes later, I showered, put on a fresh change of clothes and together we went grocery shopping.

At the local farmer's market, Johnny whistled the theme song of Mr. Belvedere. "What are we doing here?" I asked. "We're buying all the eggs." Johnny replied. That's right, we loaded one hundred dozen eggs into Johnny's Mercedes jeep and with one salute to the manager, our wholesale purchase of eggs was made. I learned that Johnny owned a small share of this particular farmer's market. (Just the eggs aisle.)

At Johnny's private vineyard; Depp Wines in Santa Barbara. There was a hot tub bang in the middle of the vineyard and Johnny quietly said, "My dear man, both compliments and insults must roll off your back as if they were the one and the same." I agreed and then popped off my shirt.

This hot tub however, was not meant for bubbling our troubles away, but being soft boiled with the one hundred dozen eggs. It was the egg cleansing ritual to teach me that compliments and insults should have no effect on my inner beauty. Also chicken eggs to Johnny were the sexiest beings on earth. Johnny sprinkled some salt in the tub and added that salt raises the boiling temperature. I explained that the tub doesn't even reach boiling temperature, so the salt doesn't do anything. Johnny smiled. He then called me, "Beautiful." I blushed and shooed his compliment away like a little girl. "You failed on that compliment. Simmer in this egg tub for three more hours." barked Johnny. Feeling safe with him, I took a nap.

Hours later, I awoke to Johnny Depp's menacing yet heroic cries. I jumped out of the tub and saw Johnny lizard running, as he does, around a two story tall replica of the Eiffel tower. Did he need my help? Was my helping him meant to be an elaborate way to help myself? And how did he look so good even when he's trying to look stupid? I jumped out of the hot tub and chased after him. "Johnny! Johnny!" I called out. He was a fast runner, but my beauty within gave me strength. He screamed, "I can't stop running until you tackle me to the ground!" I tackled him to the ground like an NFL point guard. "Are you okay?" I asked. Johnny confessed that he needed help. Already feeling twice as beautiful, I said, "Just name it man. Name it."

Johnny wanted me to play Superman while he re-enacted Lex Luthor from the Tim Burton remake of the Superman movie that was never made. "How is that going to help either of us?" I asked. "It's simple," Johnny continued, "One, I've never based a character on a newly promoted TSA officer before and two, you flying will be your final test of beauty." I volleyed, "Dude, but that's a Tim Burton movie and it never happened. Tim Burton would have used wires and ropes. Also, Tim Burton isn't..." He covered my mouth and his shoulders sank in defeat. "Oh you've done it now." "Done what?" I asked in my head. "You said Tim Burton three times." POOF! Then from a cloud of dust, Tim Burton appeared out of nowhere.

Mr. Burton stood there wearing large sunglasses, his student filmmaker hairstyle and a crooked smile. Johnny explained, "When you say Tim Burton three times, he appears out of nowhere and I have to sign a movie contract if I want him to leave." Tim Burton glanced at me and shrugged, 'yeah'.

Burton held out a five page document in front of the handsome actor. Without reading a word, Johnny signed it with a scrunched up face. A second later POOF Tim Burton vanished. I asked Johnny, "What movie did you just sign with that director?" Notice, how I didn't say Tim Burton even once? Johnny sighed, "It doesn't matter anymore. After not casting me in Big Fish, that guy can shove it."

As an apology to Johnny for summoning Tim Burton, I agreed to play Superman. I stuffed a pink towel down the back of my shirt and chased after

Johnny singing the John Williams theme song, not the Hans Zimmer one. His theme song sounded more like a hundred dozen drummers. I also didn't understand why Zod had to be a DJ and use dub step on full bass to destroy the world, but enough about Hollywood. Johnny then insisted that I go up the replica of the Eiffel tower and leap from the top. He was crazy, but so good looking and rich, I must use the words eccentric and trustworthy.

Johnny calmly announced, "Look my dear man, I know it sounds crazy, but you have to be mad. It's the only way to stay sane in a mad, mad world." Johnny then ripped his shirt off and revealed a tattoo of a butterfly. Underneath its wings, it read, 'Beauty is the acceptance to live for a day.' Once again, Johnny made complete sense and his sun-kissed chest was quite fetching. However, I didn't want to die beautiful. I wanted to live beautiful. I asked if we could do this on a smaller replica of the Eiffel tower, maybe I could draw one up on the floor. Johnny said, "Just hold my hand and we'll jump together." I looked deep into Depp's eyes. I wanted to trust him, I really did. Johnny sensed my cowardice, bailed on me and took the elevator to the second story all by himself. It tore my insides up, until the elevator got stuck. From my soul I heard Johnny's cries. "Superman, Superman! Will you save me?"

I knew what I had to do. I then closed my eyes and said, "Tim Burton, Tim Burton, Tim Burton." Johnny screamed so loud, the honeymooning Pakistani couple in the adjacent vineyard started screaming back. As Tim Burton appeared, I snatched the all-black Superman costume from his arms and put it on as fast as I could. Tim then held out a contract for me to sign. Without looking, I signed it and now will be a featured extra on his next movie. POOF. Tim Burton was gone, but Johnny's screams continued.

I shut my eyes and as love, fear, power, anger, courage entered my soul I felt a wind gather beneath my feet. A second later, I began to take off. It was a miracle. The wind in my face, I was an unstoppable force of beauty. A pigeon then crashed into my face and died. After shaking his feathers off, I went back to being beautiful and saved my mentor of beauty.

Johnny summed up his lesson. "So you see, we are all miracles of beauty waiting to embrace ourselves." I wanted to heighten this moment of beauty, but I didn't feel like peeing in my pants again. Johnny and I said our goodbyes with a hug and two perfect hair flips. Together or apart, we were poetry in motion.

You may want to stay at home in the summer of 2019. That will be the year Tim Burton's Aquaman will release in theaters and Johnny Depp will reluctantly play Aquaman's evil step brother with a lisp.

For more of this writer's work or to stay in touch, please visit CatchTwentyDu.com